Light·er

(adj.)

There are a few things in this

world that make us let go of

what made our hearts feel

heavy.

I hope

you find

one of them

and

I hope

it makes you

feel

lighter.

I've found it.

Contents

- Y_{ou} -

Be gentle

with yourself.

You,

too,

have a heart

that is in need

of your forgiveness.

— *Heavy*

You

are

the only thing

standing

in

your

way.

Move.

Let yourself through.

—— *Barricade*

You

aren't meant

to feel

empty

when

you give.

If you do

then

you are

giving

too much

of yourself

to

the wrong people.

You don't need to justify how
you feel to anyone. You are
who you are and you feel what
you feel. Anyone who can't
understand that isn't worthy of
knowing you in the first place.

Some days you will feel like

you can handle just about

anything; as if you have the

heart, mind, and courage to do

whatever life may throw at

you.

Some days you won't and that's

okay, too.

No one has the power to fix
you.

Someone comes and bandages
where it hurts for a little while,
making you believe you're
healing, but that's not their job.
You're much more complex
than being temporarily
plastered. This kind of healing
needs to come from within.

It starts with accepting that
you're a unique product of
what you've gone through.

It starts with realizing that

feeling weak doesn't make you

weak.

It starts and ends with you.

You need to do this.

No one else can do it for you.

— 23:08

Out of all the people you're

proud of,

you should be of yourself most

for knowing

exactly

what it feels like

to drown

and still

be willing

to swim.

— *Only after you've*
drowned will you
breathe for the first time

You've built a wall,

so high above you,

and forgotten

that

you

could

b.

m

i

l

c

There are these moments;

moments that make you smile a

little to yourself because you

know you're making memories.

You know right then and there

that you are always going to

remember this.

Get out,

do,

venture,

and create these moments.

You're alive,

yes,

but have you lived,

my dear?

Sometimes,

a little light

is all

you can give

a person

but

sometimes,

a little light

might be all

a person needs

when they're stranded

in the darkness

of the sea.

— *Lighthouse*

In a universe that is so vast and

so beautiful,

with infinite constellations and

wonders that our minds are yet

to comprehend, He said that

you are His greatest creation.

Yet,

you still seem to doubt that you

are special.

— Aḥsana taqueem

Let go of your worries,

let go of your past,

let go of your future,

let go of everything for a little

while.

Feel what it's like not to think

of absolutely nothing; for your

mind to be blank.

Quiet.

A heavy heart and a crowded

mind can drown you.

Be light.

Stay afloat.

— *Light*

There will be moments in the

midst of the storm, when the

tides are calm and you can see

for miles once again.

Take those moments,

hold on to them,

and let them be your shelter

when it pours.

Breathe,

listen,

there's something to gain

from the howling

of the wind,

the drizzle

of the rain.

They whisper

the secrets

of keeping you

sane.

Breathe,

listen,

there's something to be gained.

This could be the end of you

or

this could be the beginning of

you.

The choice is yours to make.

—— *Perspective*

Hold

your own hand

and

jum

p.

—— *Liberty*

Once again you are where

you've been countless times

before; doubting your own

capabilities, scared of the

oncoming.

Just keep one thing in mind:

you've been here a hundred

times, but, darling, you've

proven yourself wrong a

thousand times more.

The real advantage of today's

hardship is that you have its

lesson to get you through

tomorrow's.

Dig hard,

dig deep.

All that

you need

is within.

— *Hidden*

I beg you

to dig

a little

deeper

than flesh.

Skin cells

and limbs

can never

define

a person,

don't

allow them

to define

you.

— *Treasures*

This needs to be bigger and

that could be smaller. They've

told you this is beauty and

you've believed them.

Now, let me tell you and maybe

you'll believe me: the only

thing that needs to be bigger is

your heart and what could be

smaller is your ego. Work on

beautifying what is permanent

and not what is only

temporary.

Take a moment to

breathe in the cold morning air.

Alas, you've found home.

— *Fajr*

Be patient

and understanding

with life.

What is yours,

will come.

— *Sabr*

Let the pieces

f

  a

l

  l

where they may,

and maybe,

just maybe,

you'll like that arrangement

better than your original.

Stop

spending

your time

wishing

before

you start

wishing

you had

the time.

  — *Today*

If

you've found

someone

who is

willing

to listen

to your

2AM thoughts,

keep them around.

—— *Pieces to peace*

Learn

to speak

your body's

tongue.

It speaks to you.

Stop.

And listen.

—— *This is a two-sided*

conversation

You are not an inanimate

object.

You are not meant to sit in a

corner and look pretty while

you wait for someone to come

and admire you.

You are a woman with

ambitions, opinions and

aspirations.

They can be heard; they don't

have to always be whispered.

> —— *To the girls that still*
>
> *seem to think that they*
>
> *have one purpose in life*

My dear,

You spend your time planning

for the future.

You will soon begin to see that

the future has very different

plans for you.

— *Qadar*

You

will not

have

tomorrow

if

you're

stuckonyesterday.

— *Let it go*

Find happiness

in the innocence of children,

in the magic of clouds at sunset,

in the first w   i   f
           h   f
of freshly baked cakes,

in long, lingering hugs,

in overdue reunions,

in warm smiles on strangers'

faces.

Find Happiness in things that

will always be there, even when

you feel like there is nothing

left.

— *Noticing*

Try not to look at others and

what they are capable of doing

that you are not.

They've been down different

roads that granted them

different destinations.

Look at your heart.

It has been to war more often

than not and

yet

it stands,

wounded

36

but brave,

for another battle.

You are here now.

You've survived things that

have left others in pieces.

You're on your own road.

— *You will be granted your*

own destination

You don't need the company of

those who make you feel better

by making others feel worse.

— *Bad company*

Your mind is your worst enemy

when you are worried. It

creates illogical thoughts and

fills you with fear and

hopelessness.

It's best to remember that they

are only thoughts and

thoughts

cannot

control

you.

You control you.

— *What ifs*

You

can't

fix

the broken

unless

the broken

want

to be

fixed.

— *I've tried*

It's okay

to be a little selfish sometimes.

Every now and then,

choose yourself.

— The peace I've found in

uttering, "No."

- I -

1992,

why did you not warn me of
the days of dark hues?

> — *Recently, life has been*
> *black and white with an*
> *occasional sunset that*
> *fades too quickly*

I

sometimes think

that

the child I was

was much stronger

than the adult I am.

— *Had I known*

The innocence

of my childhood

was buried with

my

p   i   n   k

t   p s

  e   u   e

     a   c   t

in my backyard

and

I'd be willing to

dig beneath the rose bushes

to bring it back.

— *Secrets*

The laughter echoes,

a little too far away,

in the old tree house.

—— *Scarred knees*

I have,

many times,

built a home within myself.

And I have,

equally as many,

watched it crumble.

— *Dependence*

My mind

and

my heart

are at

constant battle

for whom will

destroy

me

first.

— *The war*

I close my eyes and I can see it
all. I can see when I was seven
and when I was seventeen. I
can see people I've lost touch
with, I can see places I no
longer visit, I can see moments
I wish I could relive.

The sad truth is that eventually,
that's all it'll be; just a series of
"Remember when...?" and "I
wish I could go back."

You're afraid

of the dark

yet you continue

to walk yourself

down narrow allies

after midnight.

You continue

to lose sleep.

— *Tomorrow*

The sun has set

and within the darkness

the people sleep.

The sun has set

and within the darkness

my demons creep.

—— *Midnight tea*

My body is demanding an

apology from a certain noisy

tenant that has kept it awake till

the early hours of dawn.

It is the reason it is often

restless.

The reason it often aches.

It has tried everything.

It tried to ignore it but it's far

too loud. It often shouts things

repeatedly for attention. It even

tried to distract it for maybe

it'll give but that didn't work

either.

My mind is stubborn and

demands to have its way.

—— *Control*

Key in hand,

I grew comfortable

caged in my past.

— *It's familiar here*

I am growing envious of those

who are capable of articulating

my own thoughts better than I

can.

How are you able to reach into

the depth of my heart and mind

when I am

desperately,

with all my being,

trying to touch their surface?

— *Sorcery*

57

It's **dark** again.

It's dark again and it's become a

lot harder to find the horizon.

—— *Pessimist*

I have faith.

I know that my every breath is

meant for me and every step I

take was always meant to be

mine.

But,

often,

the air thickens,

but,

often,

my legs ache.

You run,

and run,

and you tell yourself to keep

running,

you tell yourself that it's okay

to be out of breath because

in the end,

it'll be worth it.

The burning lungs,

the racing heart,

the weak legs,

the sweaty palms,

and the lack of sanity

will all be worth it.

Then,

one day,

you stumble and fall.

You catch a glimpse of what

you've left behind and you

realize,

you're back

to where

you

first

started.

— *Relapse*

How beautiful

it is

to feel things

that aren't fear.

— *12 years*

It's getting too much.

Fight.

I'm losing hope.

Fight.

I can't do it.

Fight.

I want to get out of here.

Fight.

> —— *Fight or flee (always*
>
> *fight, my dear.)*

The storm has passed,

yes,

but

what use

is a sun

with

nothing left

to shine on?

—— *Irreparable damage*

He has not failed you once.

Dear heart,

when will you learn that as long

as He's with you, you'll always

be okay?

He is with you.

Always.

In all ways.

But why

do you continue

to soak yourself

with the gasoline

of 'what'

and ignite yourself

with the match

of 'if'?

— *Panic*

The

fear

of fall

        ing

is

much

scarier

than

the fall.

How do I teach myself to be

okay with change? How do I

tell myself that everything

around me is about to be

different,

unknown,

and that I must be okay with it?

— *Comfortably dull*

I am not upset, nor bothered by

what

has come early,

has come late,

or has not come at all

for I

trust in a plan

that was written

by The Greatest Writer.

— *What You wrote for me*

is all that shall ever be.

That's where I found

peace

Last year feels like last week

and I'm afraid I'm going to look

back on my life and see that it

has all gone by

while I just sat

here,

waiting,

hoping tomorrow held my

answers.

Why

is it

that

on the coldest nights

I feel

the warmest?

— *December*

Don't let in just anyone.

Not everyone will be accepting

of the mess you've created.

Not everyone will be willing to

help you clean it up.

— *Clutter*

People don't try to figure you

out.

They just decide

what you are

by who you were

and tell you

how you should be.

—— *This town*

You're brave, to forgive,

but a fool if you forget;

a sweet, naïve fool.

The taste of serenity after the

chaos makes it almost all worth

it.

Almost.

— *But not quite*

I am

within

the stars and the galaxies

and

the stars and the galaxies

are

within me.

—— *Wander and wonder*

Is it kind

or

foolish

of me

to still believe

there is good

in everyone

despite

being proven wrong

time and time again?

— *On the verge of*

developing trust

issues

77

Ameena Karaja
Light·er

I've grown

to believe that

some people

go

to their closets

in the morning

and ask themselves,

"What mask should I wear

today?"

— *Who am I speaking*

to this time?

Tonight, the clouds scream

and I'll fall asleep, soundly

to their symphony.

I fear a lot of things, you know.

I fear elevators,

I fear distance,

I fear death.

It was never my own, though. I

fear I'll have to face a day

without you and I might not be

able to. I fear that it'll take the

life out of me while I'm still

alive.

> —— *A sleepless 11 year*
>
> *old*

Let's sit for a cup of tea while

you tell me all the stories that

made you laugh till your sides

hurt, the stories that changed

you, and the stories that broke

you.

Tell me what made you and I'll

listen.

I don't mind if my cup gets

cold.

       — Love

I often find myself channelling
parts of the ones I love to get
me through the day.

I channel my mum's
determination when I want to
give up. I channel my dad's
unapologetic personality when
being myself has left me
disliking myself. I channel my
sister's constant optimism
when I can only see the dark
sides. I channel my brother's
heart-warming kindness when
being kind is draining me. I

channel my best friend's

unwavering strength when I am

overwhelmed. I channel my

niece's carefree spirit when I

am thinking too much.

My point is, I am an

amalgamation of the incredible

souls God has blessed me with

and I can't help but think how

lucky I must be to have people

around me that others search

an entire lifetime for.

— *Who are you?*

The homes

I've built

in people

are falling

apart

and I'm

afraid

of being

homeless.

— *Debris*

It

wasn't

until

I heard

the silence

did I

realize

how loud

it had been.

— *Break or break. You*

choose

And so, she wandered;

for only by getting lost,

she could have been found.

— *The search*

Just about everyone I've met

aren't who I first met.

— *Pros and cons but*

mostly pros

She made a list of what has

upset her and promised herself

to never be those things.

She promised to be honest, she

promised to me kind, but

mainly,

she promised

not

to make

anyone

feel

as

she

has once

felt.

You trust people with parts of

you

and once they've taken what

they needed, they leave,

keeping you behind,

feeling like something's

missing.

> — *The reason why them*
>
> *leaving left you*
>
> *empty*

From the thorns that once grew

in the crevasses of your mind,

roses will,

one day,

bloom.

—— *Gardens*

Today,

the rain made me smile again
and I realized
that I'm always going to be
okay.

—— *Epiphany*

- We -

Some

are human

with a touch

of magic,

some

are human

with a touch

of tragic

and I find the latter much more

intriguing.

— *My type*

It is often

that we

destroy

ourselves

in the process

of trying

not to

destroy

others.

— *Mum*

We have the habit of picking at

our scabs,

till they bleed again,

and then

wondering

why

our old wounds

still hurt.

As human beings, from the first

day we were born, there is so

much expected from us. Be it to

say our first words, to take our

first steps, to write our names,

to ace our exams, to graduate,

to find jobs, to start families

and so on. We seldom have the

time to discover what we

expect from ourselves because

we're so caught up in trying to

satisfy other members of

society.

My dear,

breathe.

Breathe and take some time to

understand that it is okay to put

yourself first.

Take some time from

nourishing your mind to

nurture your soul.

— Over time not

overtime

Some things are better kept

inside of us.

Some things are too FRAGILE to

be placed in the unsteady hands

of others.

I genuinely hope your life is as

perfect as you're trying to make

us believe.

(Chances are, it isn't and I want

you to know that you can stop

pretending. It's safe here.)

Lay upon me your burdened

heart

and I will lay upon you mine.

We'll talk about what has left

them broken

and what has mended with

time.

A human

without

humanity

is merely

a mammal

in the food chain.

— *The id*

If

we don't

at least

try

to warm

their

cold hearts,

then

we are

partially

responsible

for

their blizzards.

— *Kindness*

Somewhere along the way, we

forgot that we are human, too.

We were never told that we are

deserving of our own honesty,

love and sympathy.

And no one teaches us that. No

one teaches us how to treat

ourselves with the same

softness we treat the ones we

love.

We are made of dirt.

We are meant to be submerged

in darkness before we can grow

from the depth of it.

— *Seeds*

There are things we only notice

when we don't want to notice:

- Time when you want it

   to pass.

- Your breathing rate

   when the air feels thick.

- When someone is gone.

Remnants of our being were

left behind with people who

have forgotten us and in places

where the evidence of our

existence was washed away by

last winter's rain.

We are dispersed,

s c a t t e r e d,

and we are yearning to be

whole again.

— Two homes

Like autumn and spring,

time took them away from you,

time shall again bring.

— *The things we've lost*

We shouldn't believe that

only by being

caressed,

bathed,

and submerged

in darkness can we bleed

crimson words on these pages.

Feelings like these should never

be romanticized.

— *Artists*

It's funny how the only way we

can keep our sanity is by not

q u e s t i o n i n g

it.

— *"Normal"*

111

The little beauty left in the

world will be obliterated by

our destructive hands,

judging eyes,

and sharp tongues.

— *News*

The same skin caresses your

bones,

as others of different tones.

I urge you to lower your pride,

if your thoughts happen to

collide.

Inhale the pain,

exhale the love.

We're all creations of

The One above.

We all have people that have
moved on without us. We all
have been through times that
have left us shattered. We are
all not where we expected
ourselves to be.

— *We're all the same.*

Some are just better

at hiding it than

others

We have a knack for fixing

what is broken then

dissecting,

analyzing,

and over analyzing

what is fixed

until it is also br

oken.

— *More to it*

Let's try not to chew on

people's words for too long.

They tend to become bitter

after a while.

— *Literal vs. Imbedded*

There are so many aspects

about us that we find ourselves

being surprised by. There are

parts of us just awaiting

discovery.

But that's the things with

treasures; you have to dig really

deep to find them.

> — *I am stronger than*
>
> *I've always thought,*
>
> *apparently (P.S. You*
>
> *probably are, too)*

Some days,

we just need the comfort of

knowing that the ones we love

will invest the

time,

love

and effort

into us as we would invest into

them.

> — *They rarely ever*
>
> *exist*

Our past consisted of us

dreaming of our futures, and,

inevitably, our future will

consist of us dwelling on our

past.

We seldom experience the

tranquility that comes with

being present in the present.

Try, for this moment, to just be

here.

Only

here.

Maybe our dreams are just that;

mere images of an unreachable

reality.

> — *The stardust on my*
>
> *dreams fell off when*
>
> *reality hit me*

There are so many

places to visit,

sunsets to photograph,

food to taste,

books to read,

and people to be kind to.

Time well spent is a life not

wasted.

Hypocrisy is advocating

forgiveness but your heart

needs it most. Hypocrisy is

telling people to be kind but

you're continuously tearing

yourself apart. Hypocrisy is

insisting there is beauty in

everything but failing to see it

within you.

And that's what most humans

are;

hypocrites.

Often,

we have to
go through something
for us to get through it.
No ways around it,
no short cuts.
Through the storm.
— *The cleansing*

Writer's Note

I thank you, dear reader, for taking the time to read my heart and my head. This collection of poetry and prose is an insight of me, my thoughts and feelings. You now know more about me than most. If you have found just one piece that you resonated with, articulated your thoughts, and ultimately made you feel *lighter*, then I am forever grateful.

When I began writing this book, my aspiration was to create a sanctuary for its readers when life weighed them down. A judgement free place, a place where they felt understood, cared for, and valued. The contents within this book got me through so much for when I write what I want to hear, I find myself at peace. I sincerely hope you find some sense of peace in here, too.

I divvied up the book into three parts; the sections of the book stem from what I find helps me stay afloat. In my experience, three kinds of words make me lighter:
The first being words of courage and empowerment which are the focus of *You*. Words that reassure me I have, I can, and I will get through this.
The second are words of understanding, of relating to someone who knows what I am going through so that I can feel a little at ease with myself; hence *I*.

The third and final words are those that make my hardships easier to cope by knowing I am not different. I am not alone. I grew up being afraid that I might stand out too much so everything I did I did with caution and constant reassurance that what I am feeling was "normal". In *We*, I want you to know there are others like you. Many more that you are not aware of.

Lastly, thank you for buying my book as for every book sold, 50% of its proceeds will go directly to support a project that is so dear to my heart - the MATW (Muslims Around The World) Project. The MATW project is a non-profit organization that serves the people of Togo, Africa. To this date, MATW has contributed to building and developing schools, mosques, houses, and water wells. One of their predominant areas of focus are the widows and orphans in Togo. You can see some their incredible work on their Instagram page: MATW_Project or visit their Facebook Page: MATW PROJECT.

So,
here I leave you,
with a sincere wish that you leave well and stay well.

Take care of your heart,
Ameena

Acknowledgments

First and foremost I thank my Creator for giving me infinite blessings and then some. I thank my family for constantly supporting and encouraging my dream of publishing my first book. Mum, Dad, Nada, Hoda, Mohammed, Ali, and Sammy, you have always believed in me, even when I didn't believe in myself. You pushed me to keep going and called me the family's Writer before it was even true. You are all my support system and I am eternally thankful for the blessing you guys are.

My friends who were always on my back to write my first book. Well, here you all go. Mabrouka Swenia, my best friend, you were the first to know about my dream and I think if it weren't for you, I wouldn't have started writing in the first place. You are probably one of the very few who understands what every single piece in this book refers to. Thank you for being there for the past ten years. Fatima Karim, thank you for always keeping an eye out for every opportunity that arose that could increase my chances of success; you're a lovely soul. Shaimaa Kraba, thank you for being a great source of knowledge and for opening my eyes to the world of writing and publishing; you are my mentor.

My instructors, especially Ms. Hala Hashem and Ms. Rasha Halat, who since the first day I attended their classes have given me words of support for everything I wrote. Their words of kindness and their belief in me has always, and will always mean so much to me. Thank you.

Thank you to my illustrator, Meream Pacayra, for painting exactly what I envisioned. (Instagram: BoredandCrafty)

A sincere thank you to everyone I didn't mention because I'd need another book to express how much you have all contributed to the making of this book. I am forever indebted to you.

About the Writer

Ameena Karaja is a Lebanese Canadian educator and writer. She has written for blogs and various published educational magazines. Her passion for helping others has led her to teaching illiterate Syrian refugees in Lebanon and dedicating her first book of poetry and prose to helping orphans and widows around the world. You can find Ameena on Instagram: AmeenaKaraja

20948682R00086

Printed in Great Britain
by Amazon